MW00964766

Beading for
Beginners

Beading for *Beginners*

Lucinda Ganderton

BARRON'S

For Gabriella Fink, with love

First edition for North America published in 2005
by Barron's Educational Series, Inc.
First published by MQ Publications limited, 2005
Copyright © 2005 MQ Publications Limited
Text copyright © 2005 Lucinda Ganderton

MQ Publications Limited
12 The Ivories, 6–8 Northampton Street
London N1 2HY
www.mqpublications.com
Editor *Katy Bevan*
Photography: *Lizzie Orme*
Illustrations: *Rachael Matthews*
Design concept: *C-B Design*

Author's Acknowledgments

Grateful thanks are due to Ljiljana and the team
at MQP: To Katy for coming up with the concept
of Beading for Beginners, her editorial expertise,
and for skillfully getting us all through to the end;
to Lindsay Kaubi (gemstone bobby pins, beaded
barrette, ice queen tiara, and loom woven
bracelet) and Jane Huckerby (rosette, turquoise
jewel bracelet, and rings) for contributing their
creative projects; to Sorrel for all her help; to
Laura and her ever-steady hands; to Lizzie (and
Charlie) for the photographs, and Viv for great
lunches; to Rachael for the innovative artwork,
and Clare for designing such an original book.

All rights reserved. No part of this book
may be reproduced in any form by photostat,
microfilm, xerography, or any other means,
electronic or mechanical, without the written
permission of the copyright owner.

All inquiries should be addressed to:
Barron's Educational Series, Inc.
250 Wireless Boulevard
Hauppauge, New York 11788
www.barronseduc.com

This book contains the opinions and ideas of the
author. The author and publisher disclaim all
responsibility for any liability, loss, or risk, personal
or otherwise, which is incurred as a consequence,
directly or indirectly, of the use and application of
any of the contents of this book.

ISBN-13: 978-0-7641-5865-0
ISBN-10: 0-7641-5865-1

Library of Congress Catalog Card No: 2005920535

Printed and bound in China
9 8 7 6 5 4 3 2 1

Contents

Introduction

Beads are bright, beautiful, glamorous, gorgeous, and, you will soon
discover, infinitely versatile. From Egyptian glass and precious stones to
contemporary shapes and modern materials, there is plenty to choose from.

Beads come in many shapes.

These charms
were collected
from exotic places.

Start to explore the amazing world of
beadwork and you will find a wealth of
glittering glass beads, gleaming pearls, and
sparkling crystals, all just waiting to be
transformed into unique projects. They can
be woven into bracelets and rings, threaded
into chokers and necklaces, or made into
earrings and brooches.

Beads are beloved by the world's top
designers, who appreciate their decorative
qualities, so beadwork is always a key trend
on the catwalk. Follow the fashionable
crowd and use beads to dress up your
clothes. You can even let beadwork
go to your head and make pretty flowered
barrettes, tiaras, and combs, all decorated
with wired beads, or add a key ring or
rosette to your best purse.

BEGINNING BEADWORK

This is an entry-level book to inspire you, and to start you off on this fascinating craft. It will guide you, step-by-step, through the basic techniques and show you how to put them into practice.

The following pages introduce the myriad beads you will encounter, show you how to thread, knot, wire, or stitch them, and teach you about the special jewelry findings and equipment needed.

INDIVIDUAL IDEAS

As you learn more about beading and acquire new skills, you can adapt the projects in this book by following the detailed instructions in the first chapter. The projects have all been designed to inspire you—change the colors to suit your own taste or pick beads to match your favorite outfit. You can then go on to develop your own ideas, to make for yourself or for your family and friends.

A piece of jewelry that has been handmade is always going to be a treasured gift and will be memorable, not just for the lucky recipient but for the maker as well.

This book makes tricky looking projects easy.

Beads come in an infinite variety of subtle colors.

handmade glass beads

Venetian beads

These glass beads are a mixture of many colors.

A WORLD OF BEADS

For such tiny objects, beads have a wealth of fascinating history. Shells, seeds, bones, and other natural objects have been strung together to make trinkets since ancient times, but the first glass beads came from Egypt, over five thousand years ago. Bead necklaces accompanied Tutankhamen to his tomb, and the method used to make them —winding molten glass around a metal core—is more or less unchanged today.

In past centuries, and in diverse cultures across the world, beads have taken on a significance far beyond their material value. They have been widely traded as a currency between nations and worn as status symbols. Spanish bullfighters, British royalty, and Native American leaders all still put on ceremonial dress that is embroidered and bedecked with beads in some form.

Millefiori beads are traditionally made in Italy.

MAGIC AND MYSTERY

Beads have long been endowed with special powers. Roman mothers put coral bracelets on their babies to ensure their continued good health, Indian maharajas sported drilled diamonds as the ultimate expression of their great power, and many religions use strings of wooden beads as an adjunct to prayer. Eye beads, with a pattern of concentric circles, were worn as protective amulets to deflect the "evil eye" by many societies and are still to be found in the street markets of the Greek islands and in the Middle East.

Ancient glass beads from the African desert.

INSPIRATIONAL IDEAS

New methods of manufacture and the development of innovative materials mean that we now have more beads and findings to choose from than ever before. Stretch bead elastic, memory wire, and tigertail wire are all ideas that have opened up new ways of putting beads together. You can buy beads from local specialty stores and craft stores, but the Internet is the truly global marketplace. You will find a list of web sites at the end of the book.

Read this book, hunt out hidden treasures, make them into your own creations, wear them, and enjoy them!

Beads &
Techniques

Beads

If you can imagine a bead, it probably exists somewhere in the world! Glass, wood, and metal beads come in every possible size, color, shape, pattern, and texture. Here are just a few of the many types you will come across once you start to explore the great diversity of beautiful beads that are out there.

lampwork Venetians

multilayered cane beads

iridescent crystal beads

GLASS BEADS

Translucent, opaque, frosted, or iridescent—there is a huge range of old and new glass beads to be found in specialty suppliers, thrift stores, craft stores, and at the bottom of your jewelry box. Venetian-style lampwork beads are among the finest: they are still crafted by hand and are embellished with trails, swirls, spots, and dots. Color may also come from applied stripes of goldstone, stripes of molten glass, or from metallic foil at the core of a transparent bead. Molded beads usually have a smooth, shiny, or matte surface, but some are ridged or angled to reflect the light.

CRYSTALS AND PEARLS

The most dazzling of all beads are multi-faceted crystals, which look spectacular when used to make large-scale projects like the Ice Queen Tiara on page 136. Czech and Austrian crystals are the most brilliant and are produced in many sizes and jewel-like colors, but vintage crystal beads have a patina of their own. They work well with faux or freshwater pearls (see the effect in the charm bracelet on page 156). Wild or cultured pearls—baroque, round, or seed shaped—are costly, but some imitations are indistinguishable from the real thing. Other pearlized beads in vibrantly bright colors make no pretense to be natural.

NATURAL MATERIALS

Large wooden beads are not just a favorite plaything of preschoolers—they can be used as the foundation for tassel heads, painted, covered with papier-mâché, or strung with rows of seed beads. Semiprecious gemstone beads or irregular tumbled chips are available from bead suppliers and can be used on their own or mixed with other, less expensive beads.

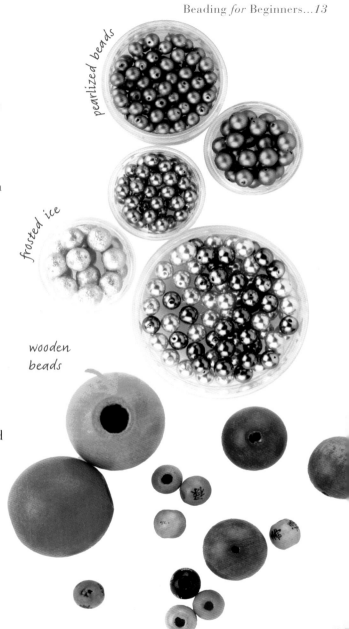

pearlized beads

frosted ice

wooden beads

Beads

Antiques

matte Delicas

large frosted
seed beads

silver-lined
seed beads

opaque
seed beads

SEED BEADS

These tiny beads, also known as rocailles,
are used for making all sorts of jewelry and
for embroidery. The smallest of all go under
the trade names of Antiques and Delicas—
short glass cylinders, with straight sides
and wide holes. They are often used for
peyote stitch—a needle weaving
technique—but are ideal for any fine
sewing, threading, or wire projects.
Rounder seed beads come in sizes from
2 mm to 5 mm (½2 inch to ⅕ inch) in
countless colors and finishes. Use them for
embroidery, loom weaving, threading, and
any designs that need small points of color,
or intricate details.

rose montees

BUGLES

Bugles are long, thin beads, cut from
drawn-out lengths of fine glass tubing.
They come in sizes from 4 mm to 4 cm
(⅕ inch to 1½ inch) and can be threaded
together or interspersed with seed beads or
larger round beads. Stitch them down to
give a geometric element to bead embroidery
or add them to beaded fringes and tassels.
Remember, however, that the ends can be
very sharp and may cut through cotton
thread, so this is not to be recommended—
always use a strong beading thread.

SEQUINS AND ROSE MONTEES

Undeniably glamorous, these sew-on
additions to beadwork will add a glitzy
touch to any project. Use them singly as
highlights within an embroidered thread or
bead design, or go all out for a rhinestone
cowboy look. Flat sequins—small disks
with holes in the center—are the most
discreet, cupped sequins are more glittery,
and other variations are stamped out in
flower or snowflake shapes. Rose montees
consist of a faceted flat-backed glass
rhinestone clipped onto metal backing. Sew
them on by passing the needle through the
cross-shaped grooves in the backing.

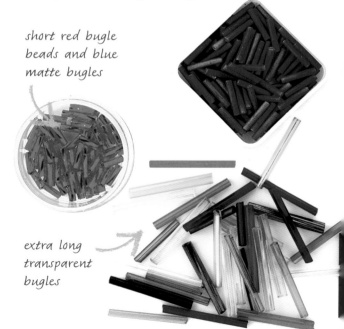

short red bugle
beads and blue
matte bugles

extra long
transparent
bugles

Findings

Clasps and findings are the useful metal loops, hooks, rings, pins, clips, and toggles that will transform a simple string of pearls or length of bead weaving into a desirable, unique piece of jewelry.

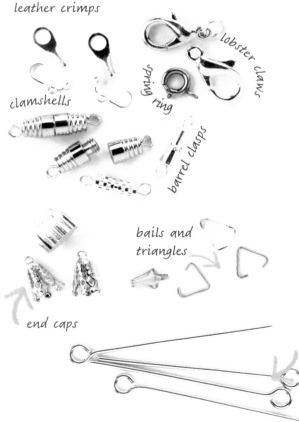

leather crimps

lobster claws

spring ring

clamshells

barrel clasps

bails and triangles

end caps

eye pins

CLASPS

Any necklace under 24 inches (60 cm) long, chokers, and most bracelets will need a clasp. These can be simple—lobster claws, spring rings, or screw clasps—or ornate—fashionable loops and toggles, antique-style box clasps, and graphically named S hooks.

A leather crimp or clamshell clasp is usually used to attach each end of the thread onto the two parts of clasp. Spacer hangers and bars are used to separate the strands of a multistranded necklace, while end caps conceal the knots of a ropelike necklace or tassel earring.

FINDINGS

Versatile jump rings—round metal loops that are opened and closed with pliers— can be found in almost all jewelry projects, linking earrings to fittings, charms to chains, or clamshells to clasps.

Wire triangles, or metal bails, are used instead of jump rings on drop beads with a tapered top. Thread beads onto straight wire eye pins or head pins to make earrings, then hang them from stud backings, fishhooks, or kidney loops. Really elaborate earrings can be made by wiring beads onto perforated clips.

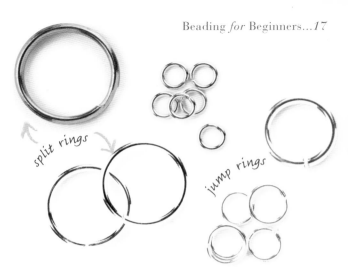

split rings

jump rings

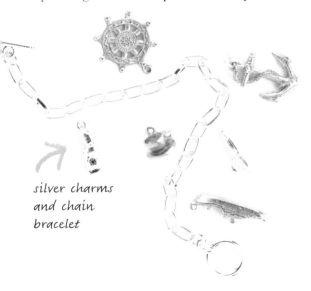

silver charms and chain bracelet

OTHER SUPPLIES

These are the invaluable bits and pieces that do not fit under the other headings. Crimp beads are ringlike metal beads used to join two ends of thread or to space beads along wire or monofilament. Attachments to make eyeglass holders are made from silicone or neoprene. Secure one onto each end of a string of beads and you will never mislay your sunglasses again. Safety pins are not just for fixing broken zippers— add a few beads and they make great friendship charms. And, finally, barrettes and bobby pins can be embellished with beads to make pretty hair accessories.

Threads and Wire

Choose a thread to match the weight and size of the beads that you are using—anything from almost invisible fine monofilament to chunky leather cord. Wire, too, comes in various thicknesses and can be surprisingly colorful.

THREADS

Multistrand nylon Nymo is specially produced for beading. It comes in different thicknesses and colors and can be threaded through a needle (flatten the cut end between finger and thumb first and use a long-eyed needle) for weaving and threading projects. Springier plastic monofilament may be opaque or clear— a quality that makes the beads appear to float—and is ideal for needle weaving or threading necklaces of smaller beads. Stretch jewelry cord or elastic is fun to use, passes easily through beads, and is used widely for snap bracelets and friendship rings. The heaviest beads can go onto leather or suede laces or round cord, which works well with ceramic, stone, or natural wooden beads. Shiny satin cord (known, rather gruesomely as rattail) is also good for large beads, and pearl embroidery thread is pretty for threading as well as sewing.

Nymo threads

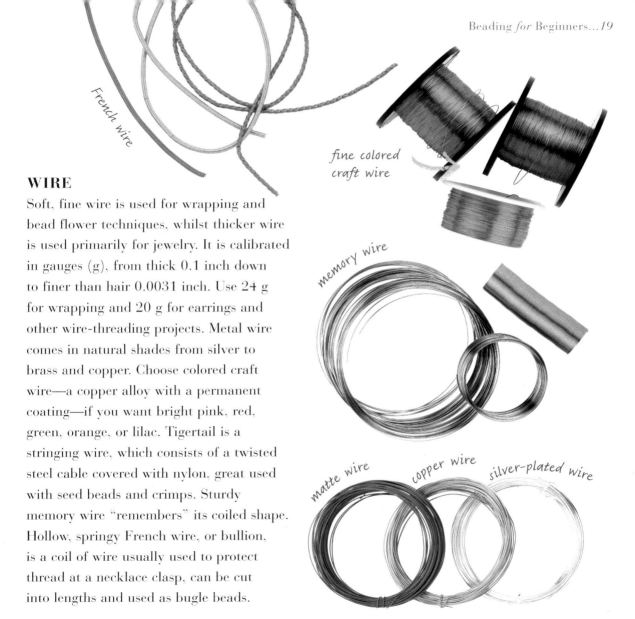

French wire

fine colored
craft wire

memory wire

matte wire   copper wire   silver-plated wire

WIRE

Soft, fine wire is used for wrapping and
bead flower techniques, whilst thicker wire
is used primarily for jewelry. It is calibrated
in gauges (g), from thick 0.1 inch down
to finer than hair 0.0031 inch. Use 24 g
for wrapping and 20 g for earrings and
other wire-threading projects. Metal wire
comes in natural shades from silver to
brass and copper. Choose colored craft
wire—a copper alloy with a permanent
coating—if you want bright pink, red,
green, orange, or lilac. Tigertail is a
stringing wire, which consists of a twisted
steel cable covered with nylon, great used
with seed beads and crimps. Sturdy
memory wire "remembers" its coiled shape.
Hollow, springy French wire, or bullion,
is a coil of wire usually used to protect
thread at a necklace clasp, can be cut
into lengths and used as bugle beads.

Tools

Most beadwork and jewelry making requires little in the way of specialized equipment—you will already have some of it in your workbox—but as you become less of a beginner, you can invest in a pair of pliers, wire cutters, and a loom.

bent nose pliers

round nose pliers

wire cutters

PLIERS

The serious beader will have three pairs, but you can start off with just bent nose pliers, which opens or closes rings and bends wire easily with its smooth jaws. You can then go on to buy round nose pliers for making perfect loops or a pair of bent nose pliers for bending or twisting wire and holding work in progress, while working on it with the other hand. Special nylon-coated pliers will not damage precious metals or beads while working. Wire cutters will slice cleanly through both wire and tigertail.

nylon jaw flat nose pliers

tape measure

sharp scissors

SEWING TOOLS

Embroidery scissors with narrow, sharp blades are useful for snipping thread, elastic, ribbon, and knots. Keep your sewing scissors for fabric only—the blades will soon blunt on paper, and wire ruins them! A measuring tape is handy for cutting accurate lengths of thread and for checking how quickly your necklace or woven bracelet is progressing. Fine sewing needles can be used for all but the tiniest beads. Sharps, or quilting needles have round eyes that are good for monofilament, and embroidery needles are best for Nymo or polyester thread. The most common sizes for beading needles are 10, 11, 12, and 13—the higher the number the finer the needle.

ADHESIVES

Super glue is helpful for securing knots: To stop them from unraveling, put a small blob on the center before clipping the ends. A coat of glue or nail polish on the end of a thread will stiffen it enough to pass through a bead without a needle. Clear adhesive tape can be temporarily used as a stopper when threading beads and is good for picking up stray seed beads from the carpet.

LOOM WEAVING

A bead loom is essential for loom weaving projects. Don't be put off by its technical appearance—it is easy to thread up and to use. Bead weaving requires special wirelike needles, which are very long, thin, and flexible.

beading loom

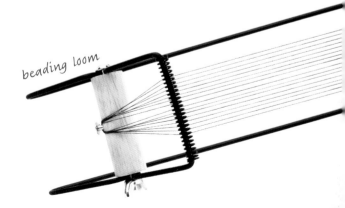

Stringing

Stringing beads is something we can all do—it is one of the first skills that small children learn in nursery school—so the creative aspect comes in when you decide exactly which beads you are going to put together, in what order, and on what type of thread.

silver-lined seed beads

SEED BEADS

Stringing these tiny beads needs a little patience, but you will be rewarded with a lovely necklace. Pass a fine thread through a fine (size 10 and up) needle. Thread the first bead to 2 inches (5 cm) from the other end, and loop the thread back through the bead again to secure. Tip the beads into a shallow container, then pick them up, a few at a time, with the point of the needle.

RIBBON

Glass beads look luxurious if they are threaded on fine silk or organza ribbon. Simply trim the end to a narrow point and pass it through the hole. If the ribbon is too thick to do this, use a needle threader. Push the wire loop through the bead and slip the ribbon through the hole. Pull the threader back through the bead and slip the bead as far down the ribbon as you wish.

THREAD AND YARN

It is not always easy to persuade a frayed end of yarn to go through a small hole, so follow my mother's favorite trick to thread beads onto yarn. Thread a needle with fine thread and knot the ends to form a loop. Pass 12 inches (30 cm) of yarn through the loop, then thread on the beads, pushing them along the fine thread and onto the yarn.

ELASTIC

Bead elastic is great for bracelets because
they allow the bracelet to slip on easily.
To make this double-stranded version,
thread a large confetti bead onto a 20-inch
(52 cm) length of elastic with a needle,
then add three seed beads and a bugle in
a repeating pattern until it fits your wrist.
Repeat for the next round, passing the
needle through every sixth seed bead.
Join the ends with a crimp.

BUTTONS AND BEADS

These natural partners can be threaded
on a double strand of fine monofilament
so that they appear suspended in midair.
Pass both ends through a bead, then
through the two holes of a button, one
from back to front and the other from
front to back. Repeat these two steps to
the end, then add a clasp to make a quirky,
and fashionable, necklace.

SILKEN STRANDS

Semiprecious gemstone beads and delicate pearls need extra special care. They are traditionally threaded onto lustrous twisted silk, which comes in many subtle colors, complete with a wire needle at the end. A small knot is tied between each bead, to stop them rubbing together and getting damaged. It is also a good way to stop the beads from rolling off if the necklace snaps.

Push the knot close to the bead using a needle.

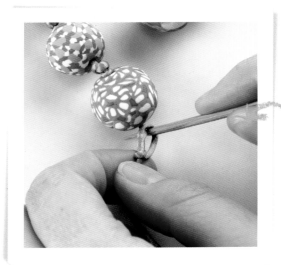

KNOTTED STRANDS

Here, on a larger scale, is how to make the knots on a strand of handmade clay beads. Make an overhand knot, close to the last bead threaded, and insert a toothpick or needle through the loop. Use this to slide the knot back along the thread until it lies next to the bead; then, keeping the tension, pull up the loose end to tighten the knot so that it resembles a small bead.

Clasps

Any necklace that cannot be put on over your head needs a clasp to join the two ends together, as do chokers, bracelets, and belts. Some of these can be as decorative as the beads themselves, while others are so unobtrusive that you hardly notice they are there.

LEATHER CRIMP

This specialized eyelet secures a clasp to a leather cord. Slip it onto the cord so that the open metal loop is level with the end, then squeeze it shut with pliers so that it grips on to the cord. You can then use a jump ring to attach a clasp through the hole. These are also known as lace-end crimps, as they can be used on any suede laces or round, woven cord.

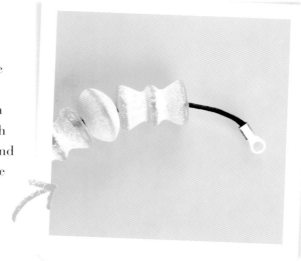

leather cord with a hook and eye clasp

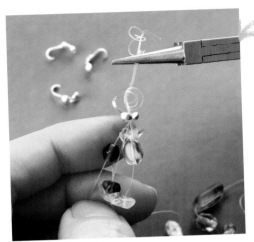

Pliers will also help tame multi-strands when knotting together.

CLAMSHELL

A clamshell is a useful small finding, designed to neaten the ends of a strand of beads. A hinged metal sphere, it has a hole at the bottom and a hook, which bends into a loop for the clasp, at the top. Pull the threads up through the hole and knot them tightly. Secure with super glue and clip the ends. Squeeze the two sides of the clamshell together gently, using flat nose or crimping pliers to close.

CRIMP AND CLAMSHELL

Rigid tigertail cannot be knotted like monofilament, so use this method to secure it within a clamshell. Before you thread any beads, pass the ends of the wire through a crimp, and squash it with flat nose or crimping pliers. Trim the ends with wire cutters. Slip the loose ends through a clamshell and squeeze it shut over the crimp. When you have finished, thread on a clamshell, then crimp the ends.

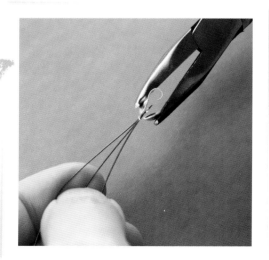

Clasps

SQUEEZING A CRIMP

As well as being used to hold wires together, crimps make useful spacers. Set one on either side of a bead, to keep it in a fixed position on a wire or thick thread. This picture shows just how to squeeze a crimp in place. Use pliers with smooth inner jaws and close them gently to flatten the crimp so that it grips the wire firmly.

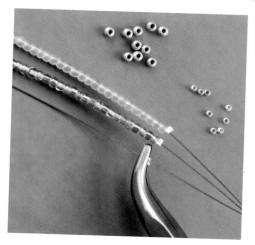

Bent nose pliers are easy to use.

JUMP RING

Jump rings link clamshells to clasps. Choose the smallest ring possible—¼ inch (65 mm) or less in diameter—in a finish to match the other findings. Open it with flat nose pliers and your finger and thumb, twisting it sideways so it does not distort. A thick ring will need two pairs of pliers. Slip the fastening onto the ring, then slip the ring onto the clamshell's loop. Twist back to close.

LOBSTER CLAW CLASP

This descriptively named snappy clasp opens and closes with a spring-loaded lever. It comes in three sizes, a gold or silver finish, and is discreet enough to use on any type of necklace or bracelet. First neaten the two ends with a clamshell. Thread a jump ring through the small hole at the bottom of the clasp, then fix it to the clamshell. Attach a jump ring to the other end.

Spring rings are similar to lobster claws.

BARREL CLASPS

Also called torpedoes, the two parts of these streamlined metal clasps screw together. Slip one-half onto the thread before you put on the beads, hole first, then tie one or more overhand knots at the end of the thread. Trim and glue the knot and slide the clasp back up the thread to hide the knot. At the other end, push the knot back into the clasp with a needle.

Wire Findings

Head pins and jump rings are incredibly versatile and come in several weights, sizes, and finishes. They are not expensive, so if you plan to do a lot of jewelry making, keep a selection in your craft drawer so you can put your new ideas straight into practice.

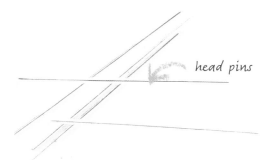

head pins

THREADING A HEAD PIN

Head pins are straight lengths of wire with a round stopper, like the head of a dressmaker's pin, molded at one end. Thread a few beads along the shaft, then bend the top into a loop to make an instant drop earring, charm, or pendant. If the stopper is too small to hold back the first bead, thread on a small seed bead to keep it in place.

ADORNING AN EYE PIN

Similar to head pins, but with a loop at the bottom end instead of a stopper, these are excellent for making more elaborate earrings. Use round nose pliers to ease the loop open, then slip on a pendant bead, drop bead, or, as here, a few small Indian-silver charms. Twist the loop back to close, then thread some more beads onto the shaft of the pin.

MAKING THE LOOP

Grasp the end of the pin with round nose pliers, about halfway down the jaws, depending on the size of the loop. Slowly roll the pliers forward, keeping the wire tight against the jaws. When the circle is almost complete, center the loop by bending the wire backward with the tip of the pliers. Slide the pin to the end of the jaws and bend them gently around to close the loop.

The loop will be the same size as the nose of the pliers.

Wire Findings

ADDING A JUMP RING

Fit a small jump ring through the top loop to make it into a drop that can then be attached onto a bracelet or earring. Softer rings may be opened by twisting one side gently forward between the finger and thumb of each hand; otherwise, use pliers. Try not to force it from the center or it will never be a perfect circle again.

Drops can be added to a charm bracelet.

USING A JUMP RING

To add beads or silver charms onto a bracelet, slip the opened ring through the small loop at the top. Slip the ring onto a link of the chain, picking it up with the pliers if you find this easier than using your fingers, then close it back up as before. Add a charm to each link, or every other link, depending on their size and the look you wish to achieve.

TRIANGLES

A jump ring would not fit through the pointed tip of a tear-drop shaped bead, so a bail, or wire triangle, is used instead. Ease the two long sides apart, this time from the center, until the space between them is just wide enough to go over the top of the bead. Position the triangle so one side is at each end of the hole, then squeeze it closed with flat nose or bent nose pliers.

EARRING FINDINGS

French ear wires, or hooks, post stud backings (for pierced ears), and screw-on posts (for non-pierced ears) have a small round loop on the underside. Just before you close the loop on your drop, slip it through this loop. If the pendant has a distinct front and back, make sure it is facing the right way around, then close the loop with pliers.

Wire Beading

Wire introduces an exciting third dimension to your beading. With the aid of a pair of pliers and some sharp cutters, you can create solid sculptural shapes such as flowers and branches, delicate jewelry, or bind beads onto other accessories to make quirky tiaras and headbands.

FRENCH WIRE

This wiggly wire is actually a narrow tightly coiled wire spring used in embroidery and to protect threads at points of high stress such as clasps. Generally only available in gold and silver colors, it can be cut into short beadlike lengths and threaded with a few special beads to turn them into a necklace or bracelet. Hold the wire cutter at right angles to the wire and snip cleanly between the coils.

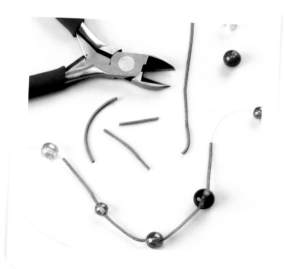

Also known as spaghetti wire, gimp, or bullion, French wire can be found in embroidery stores.

Wire and leather make a good-looking combination.

WIRING LEATHER

Soft, flexible copper wire can be wound around a thick leather cord to make a hanging loop. Slip one end through a split ring and fold back the bottom 1 inch (25 mm). Bend one end of the wire at a right angle and lay this along the short end of the leather. Wrap the long end several times around the cord, pulling it up with pliers. Clip the end and bend it back under the coil to finish.

WIRED BEADS

Turn a few single beads into a special piece of jewelry by linking them together on individual wires. Make one end into a loop as shown on page 31 and thread on the first bead. Clip the other end to ⅓ inch (8 mm) and twist it into another loop, facing the opposite direction. Wire another bead in the same way and slip the first bead onto the bottom loop before it is closed.

Monroe County Library System
Monroe, Michigan 48161

MEMORY WIRE RING

Hardened steel memory wire comes in three widths, designed to make rings, bracelets, or chokers. You will need heavy-duty wire cutters to cut the coils, as it is of industrial strength. With a bit of effort, however, you can make a small loop with round nose pliers at either end of a ring length to secure the beads and to prevent the wire from scratching the wearer.

MEMORY WIRE NECKLACE

Another way to keep the beads on the wire is to use specially produced stoppers—small silver beads with a hole that only extends halfway through the center, as used on this frosted glass necklace. Glue these onto each end of the wire with strong adhesive, and, to be sure the beads stay put, glue the first and last three beads to the wire as well.

WRAPPED HEADBAND

This effective technique is a good way to cover bangles, headbands, or napkin rings with densely packed beads. Thread the beads, allowing a few extra onto the reel of wire, then secure the loose end to one end. Wrap the wire neatly around the headband, using the teeth to space the coils, so the beads lie in neat rows along the top. Fasten the remaining wire to the other end to complete.

TWISTED BRANCHES

Twisting beads onto wire is a free-form approach which you can interpret as you wish. Start by threading three large beads onto a 12-inch (30-cm) length of colored wire, then twist the ends together into a stem. Thread on another three smaller beads, leave a 1-inch (25-mm) space, and twist another stem. Continue to make a branch, then wire the branches together.

pearlized beads and colored wire

Needle Weaving

Weaving without a loom: This free-form technique allows you to build up pieces of flat beadwork or strands of interlinked flowers, using just a tub of beads, a length of thread, and sometimes a needle. These simple patterns are just the first steps.

These rings are threaded with two strands of thread.

SIMPLE BRACELET

Thread a small bead to the center of a 20-inch (52-cm) length of bead elastic. Add a larger bead on either side, then pass both ends of the elastic through another small bead. Pull them up to form a square. Add another large bead to each end, then repeat the two steps until you have the required length. Pass one end through the first bead and secure both ends with a crimp.

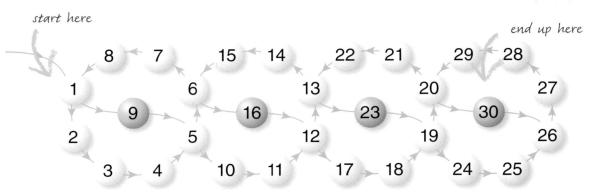

start here

end up here

SIMPLE DAISY CHAIN

This dainty flower weave is often used for little girls' rings and bracelets. It can be worked in the tiniest Delicas, as shown here, or larger round beads for a chunky look.

Use a needle to thread blue beads 1–8 onto Nymo. Take it back through 1 to make a loop. Add on yellow 9 to make the flower center and go across and down through 5. Thread on white 10 and 11, blue 12 and 13, white 14 and 15, and go back down through 6. Add yellow 16 for the next center; then repeat this sequence until you have enough for a bracelet, a choker, or a chain to hold eyeglasses.

Colors show off the shape of the flowers in this simple chain.

We used four different colors and sizes of beads.

DAISY NECKLACE

Once you have learned the basics, you can create all kinds of strands using different beads. Practice on this necklace, then try out your own ideas. Start by threading a 30-inch (76-cm) length of Nymo twice through a small seed bead as a stopper 2 inches (5 cm) from the end. Add another pink bead, five white seed beads, and an oval bead. Take the needle back through the first white bead.

MAKING A DAISY

To complete the daisy, add another three white seed beads, then slide the needle back through the final white bead of the first series (the last one before the oval center bead) to make a circle. Pull the thread up gently and you will have made the first flower.

THREADING THE SPACER

Now thread the first set of larger beads that lie between the daisies. You can use any symmetrical arrangement or copy this one by threading a tiny pink seed bead, an oval bead, a large pink faceted bead, another oval bead, and a second tiny pink seed bead. Start the next daisy with five white seed beads and an oval center and complete it as for the first flower.

FINISHING OFF

Continue weaving until you are happy with the length, ending with a complete daisy, and then thread on a clamshell and a tiny seed bead. Take the thread back through the petals of the final daisy to strengthen the end, then through the clamshell again. Knot it off, trim the end, and close the clamshell. Unpick the bead from the other end, and finish in the same way; then add a clasp (see page 29).

Fringes and Tassels

If you look around the designer stores, fringes and tassels can be found adorning just about everything from curtain tiebacks and lamp shades to evening bags. Use them to give an air of glamour and frivolity to your accessories—they are fun and easy to make.

bag charm
(see page 140)

LOOPED TASSEL

Thread a fine needle with Nymo and secure both ends to a big jump ring. Add on two large beads for the head, then about 4 inches of smaller beads in similar colors. Pass the needle up through the large bead, over the jump ring, and back down through the large beads. Continue until you have around ten loops and fasten off, gluing the threads to make sure they are secure.

BASIC FRINGE

Every strand in this straight fringe is the same length, but you could create a zigzag edge by increasing, then decreasing the amount of beads in each. Thread on twelve green and three silver seed beads. Take the needle back through the green beads so that the small beads form a stopper, and insert it at the starting point. Come out one bead's width along and repeat to the end.

SEED BEADS AND BUGLES

Mixing bead types gives a more elaborate effect. Start with one 3-mm seed bead, a bugle, one 3-mm and three 2-mm seed beads (for the stopper). Go back through the 3-mm seed bead and the bugle. The second strand starts with two seed beads, the third with three, and the fourth with four. After this, use one less seed bead in each strand until there is just one, and repeat these seven strands to form the zigzag.

LOOPS

This thicker fringe is ideal for projects that require a heavier border. Bring the needle out at the edge of the fabric and thread on the beads, remembering that you will need twice the finished length. Take the needle back into the fabric so that the last bead is next to the first. Continue making loops along the edge, each with the same number of beads, and alternating the colors.

DOUBLE LOOPS

This is a decorative fringing. Leaving a space between the start and end points of the strand creates a more open fringe. This vintage-style edging is made by sewing beads directly onto a ribbon braid. Starting at one corner, thread on five 3-mm seed beads and make two tiny stitches into the braid, $\frac{1}{3}$ inch along. Repeat to the end, then work a second row in the same spaces, this time with loops of seven beads.

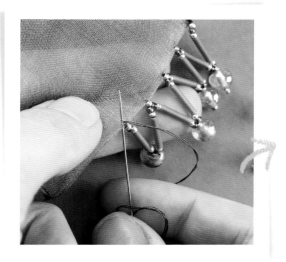

ZIGZAGS

Start off this angular fringe with three seed beads, one long bugle, and three more seed beads, then add a round bead and another seed bead. Take the needle back up through the round bead and repeat the first sequence for the second leg of the V. Secure with two small stitches, ½ inch (13 mm) along the edge. Continue to the end, starting each strand by going through the final bead of the previous V.

TEARDROP ZIGZAGS

Take the last idea one step further and you can create this pretty fringe with drop beads. Start with one seed bead, one bugle, one seed bead, one bugle, one seed bead, a pear-shaped bead, and another seed bead. Go back up through the last two beads and add one bugle, one seed bead, one bugle, and one seed bead. Secure the thread ⅓ inch (8 mm) along the edge, then go through the final seed bead to begin the next V.

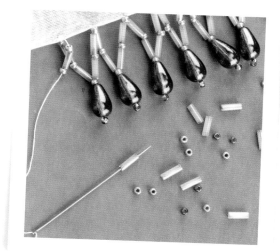

Embroidery

Small beads—both seed beads and bugles—are ideal embellishments for stitchery, whether used alongside embroidery stitches, on their own to outline shapes and highlight details within a patterned fabric (as below), or to create designs, monograms, and motifs.

Faceted beads catch the light.

SEWING SINGLE BEADS

Bring the needle up through the fabric, thread on the bead, then go back down the bead's width away from the start. Make a second stitch through the bead. You may find you can work more quickly when the beads are close to your needle. Press a circle of reusable putty adhesive into the beads and keep this on the surface of the fabric. Pick the beads off with the needle, one at a time, as you sew.

COVERED BUTTONS

Single seed beads can be packed together for maximum impact. Here they have been stitched onto a fabric-covered button, ready to decorate a jacket or cushion or to be made into a choker or pair of earrings. To cover a button follow the manufacturer's instructions, using a circle of fabric and thread that blend with the chosen beads. Starting at the center, stitch the beads on in a spiral, as closely as possible, until you reach the outside edge.

self-cover buttons

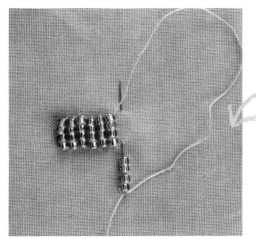

Satin stitch is a great way to block areas in one color.

SATIN STITCH

This is a quick way to sew parallel rows of small beads to make bands of color. Starting at one corner, thread on up to five seed beads (more than this and the beads will be too loose). Lay the thread across the fabric and take the needle down at the edge of the final bead. Make the next and subsequent rows in the same way, leaving the width of a bead between each one.

SURPRISING SURFACES

Once you have started to embroider with beads, you will find yourself surrounded by accessories, clothes, and pieces of fabric that just cry out for extra ornament. Beads can be sewn onto virtually anything that a needle can be pushed through—always protect your fingertip with a thimble when sewing onto thicker materials, such as this clear plastic beach sandal. The knots have been reinforced with clear glue.

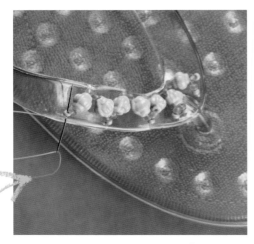

Use a strong sewing needle to pierce this plastic sandal.

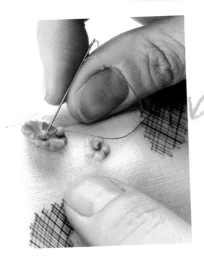

BUTTONS AND BEADS

Most of us can stitch on a button with sewing thread, but for a less utilitarian look, try anchoring them down with seed beads. These pretty, flowery buttons were part of a garden embroidery, but plain round ones would be just as effective. Bring the needle up through the hole, thread on a bead, then go down through the hole. Repeat once or three times, depending on the button.

OVERLAPPING SEQUINS

Flat sequins—the round variety with a small hole in the middle—can be sewn down singly with straight stitches worked from the center outward. Make several in a star-shaped arrangement for a starbust effect. To hide the thread completely when sewing them down in straight or curved lines, they are usually arranged in an overlapping row, like fish scales. Take the needle down at the edge of the first sequin and come up a sequin's width away.

Sew a shiny seed bead in each hole of a paillette.

SEQUINS AND BEADS

A more ornamental way to sew on a round or shaped sequin with a single hole is by anchoring it with a small seed bead. Bring the needle through, thread on the sequin and the bead, then take the needle back down through the hole. Larger round or shaped sequins, known as paillettes, have two or more holes close to the outside edge. Sew a small seed bead through each of these to secure them.

Knotting

There are two kinds of knots: functional and decorative. The art of decorative knotting —macramé—often incorporates glass or wooden beads, and it is undergoing something of a revival at present. The surfer's bracelet overleaf will give you a taste of the technique.

LARK'S KNOT

One of the simplest and prettiest knots, a lark's knot can be used to turn a large flat bead (sometimes known as a doughnut bead, because of its shape) into a choker or pendant. Choose a shiny satin cord or a round leather cord and fold it in half. Thread the loop through the center of the bead and pull the two ends up through the loop to hold it in place. Knot the ends to the required length.

Use pretty ribbon or cord to show off a special bead for a simple necklace.

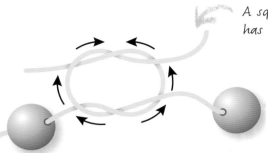

A square knot has many uses.

A slipknot is quick and easy to undo.

SQUARE KNOT

A very useful knot, this is also known as a reef knot. Use it to tie two ends together, whether to join a long necklace or to add on an extra length of thread when weaving. It is made in two steps. Pass the right thread over and under the left, then pass the left thread over and under the right. Secure with a dab of super glue, if necessary, before trimming the ends.

TIP BOX

❋ The square knot is a firm knot that will not slip. Children are taught to remember it by chanting "Right over left and under, left over right and under."

SLIPKNOT

This is a temporary knot, which can easily be undone. Before you start to thread a necklace, you should make a slipknot about 2 inches (5 cm) from the end. This can then be undone, leaving enough thread to secure the beads onto a clamshell or other clasp. Follow the diagram to see how the knot is formed. Pull the loop in the direction shown to tighten, and pull the tail to undo.

SPACING WITH KNOTS

Thread beads at intervals on fine string, cord, or a leather strip, keeping each bead in position with a single overhand knot. Several strands will make a bead curtain. This decorative alternative to a net panel or screen door adds an air of the exotic to any interior and may also be used as a room divider or screen. Drill a row of holes in a wooden pole, knot each strand through a hole, and screw to the top of the door or window.

Use a sharp point to position the knot close to the bead.

OVERHAND KNOT

This is really the simplest knot and is useful for lots of applications in beading. Use it to stop beads rolling off the end of your thread when stranding or to space the beads apart. Used between beads, it will prevent them from rubbing against one another and also stop them from rolling away should the strand ever break. This is particularly important when threading precious stones or pearls.

USING TWO STRANDS

This interesting variation on a threaded
necklace makes a silky cord into a design
feature. Thread a button halfway along
an 80-inch (2-m) length of silk thread, or
embroidery floss, and make an overhand
knot just below the button. Thread a bead
onto one strand, then make another knot,
leaving ¼ inch (7 mm) on either side of
the bead. Continue to the required length,
then finish with a loop to fasten.

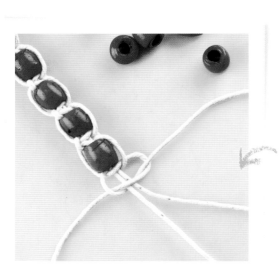

*This uses simple square
knots separated by beads.*

MACRAMÉ BRACELET

Knot two 35-inch (90-cm) lengths of string
with an overhand knot, one-third of the
way down. Pin the loop down and thread
both short ends through a bead. For the
first part of the flat knot, lay the strand on
the left across the two center strands, just
below the bead. Pass the other strand under
this thread and behind the center strands,
then through the loop on the left. Pull up
gently and repeat in the opposite direction.

Making Beads

Once you have tried out some of the techniques in the other chapters, you might like to try making some beads of your own. Children, in particular, will love the cut straws and paper beads, to which you can add painted pasta shapes, such as macaroni or penne tubes.

millefiori beads

CUT STRAWS

Plastic drinking straws come in bright colors and are ideally suited to simple bead-threading projects. Use a pair of scissors to cut them into lengths from ½ inch (13 mm) to 1½ inches (4 cm), angling the blades at right angles to the straw so that the ends are straight. The "beads" can then be threaded onto string and interspersed with bright plastic beads and paper beads.

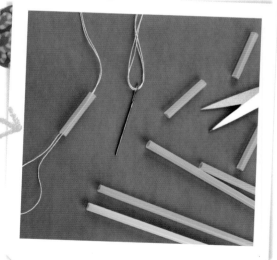

PAPER BEADS

This is a truly eco-conscious project. You can recycle anything from gift wrap to glossy magazine pages or even old letters into long, barrel-shaped beads. These examples are made from Japanese origami paper printed with delicate patterns of flowers and leaves.

Cut the paper into long, equilateral triangles, each 6 inches (15 cm) long with a 1½-inch (4-cm) base. Wrap a garden stick or thick knitting needle with a layer of plastic wrap to prevent the beads from sticking. Starting at the base, wrap each triangle around the stick, coating the wrong side with a thin layer of white glue as you roll it around. Apply a final protective coat of glue as a seal and varnish, then let it dry completely. Slide the beads off the stick and pull out the plastic wrap.

Use white glue that will dry to a clear sheen.

POLYMER CLAY BEADS

Polymer clay, marketed under various names, is an easy-to-use, malleable, synthetic clay that comes in many colors. To make a basic bead, break off a small amount, roll it between your palms until it forms a ball, then push a round wooden skewer through the center to make a hole. Slide off the bead, and bake it in the oven, according to the manufacturer's instructions.

MARBLED BEADS

You can blend polymer clay very easily to make a huge range of new colors. Knead small lumps of different clays together until they are completely blended to create your own shades, or stop the mixing process halfway to give a multicolored marbled look. These small beads are made by threading pea-sized balls of clay onto thick wire to create the holes.

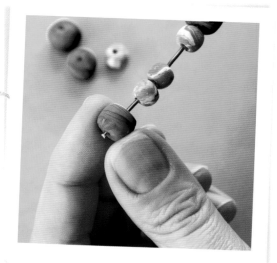

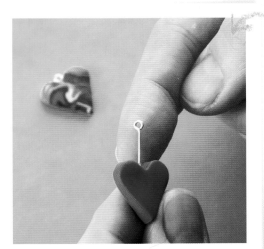

Make your own pendants with
polymer clay and an eye pin.

CUTOUT BEADS

To make small pendants, roll out a lump of
clay with a rolling pin to a depth of about
$\frac{1}{8}$ inch (3 mm). Use tiny gelatin or cookie
cutters to stamp out a shape—a star, heart,
or flower—from the clay, or cut out a motif
using a craft knife. Cut the end off an eye
pin with wire cutters, so that it is about
$\frac{2}{3}$-inch (17-mm) long, and push the blunt
end into the clay until just the loop is visible.

PIN BEADING

This is not strictly a bead-making
technique, but these glittering balls—
made by studding polystyrene balls with
beads and sequins—are so attractive that
they have to be mentioned somewhere!
Thread a seed bead onto a short beading
pin, add a sequin, and push it into the ball.
Repeat until the surface is completely
covered, overlapping each sequin slightly
over its neighbors.

These pin-beaded balls
make great decorations.

Around the
Globe

Safety Pin
Bracelet

 Deceptively simple to put together, this chunky

bracelet combines SPARKLING BEADS and

utilitarian safety pins. Jewelry like this is widely made in

South Africa, where innovative beading is a long tradition.

*Start collecting
those safety pins.*

YOU WILL NEED

Beads:
2 large crimp beads
100 x 4 mm dark red faceted beads
100 x 4 mm light red faceted beads
28 g 3 mm gold silver-lined seed beads

Findings:
50 x 1 inch silver safety pins
50 x 1 inch colored safety pins

or
100 x 1 inch silver safety pins
2 large crimp beads

Equipment:
36 inches (1 m) cord elastic
scissors
super glue
flat or bent nose pliers

A touch of glamor from the southern hemisphere.

How to make a Safety Pin *Bracelet*

Place the saftey pins head to tail.

1. Open up a silver pin, thread ten seed beads onto the point, then fasten it securely. Do the same with the other silver pins. Thread four dark or light red beads on each of the colored pins.

2. Cut the elastic in half. Make a slipknot (see page 49) at one end of each length. Thread a silver pin onto one piece, through the bottom loop, then add a colored pin through the hole in the head of the pin. Continue until all the pins are on the elastic, alternating the silver and colored pins, and placing them head to tail.

A new lease
on life for
the humble
safety pin.

③ Undo the slipknot, then slipknot the two ends together to make a circle. Thread the second length of elastic through the remaining loops and clasps. When you have finished, undo the slipknot.

TIP BOX

❈ Single beaded safety pins make sweet gifts, or friendship tokens, which can be threaded onto cords, shoelaces, or tied in small bunches as a zipper pull.

④ Pass both ends of the elastic through a crimp bead. Pull them up so there are no spaces between the pins, making sure that the elastic is not stretched. Put a blob of glue over the join and squeeze the crimp with pliers. Let it dry, then trim the ends. Finish the other ends in the same way.

Venetian Bead
Bracelet

These beautiful **MILLEFIORI BEADS** have been made on the Venetian island of Murano for centuries: Threading them onto a coil of memory wire gives them a modern, *new look* and is easy to do.

Millefiori Venetian beads are made with long canes of glass.

YOU WILL NEED

Beads:
14 x 6 mm amber glass rainbow beads
13 x 12 mm-diameter flat Venetian
    glass beads

Findings:
bracelet memory wire

Equipment:
wire cutters
bent or round nose pliers

*Millefiori means
"a thousand flowers."*

How to make a Venetian Bead *Bracelet*

Memory wire

This wire remembers its shape.

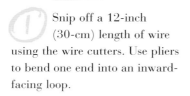

Snip off a 12-inch (30-cm) length of wire using the wire cutters. Use pliers to bend one end into an inward-facing loop.

2 Thread on a rainbow bead, followed by a Venetian bead. Add another rainbow bead, then another large bead.

TIP BOX

❋ If you have a longer length of memory wire, try making a longer bracelet with several loops and, of course, more beads.

3 Continue in this way, adding small and large beads, until they are all threaded onto the wire.

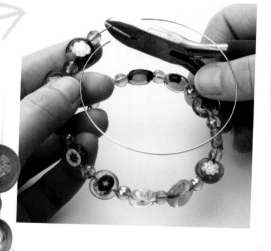

4 Clip the end of the wire to ⅓ inch (8 mm) and bend it into a loop with the pliers. Ensure that this loop also faces inward.

Magic Charm
Brooch

Put together all the *tiny charms* and pendants you have collected over the years to make a MAGICAL brooch. This is a very individual project: Take inspiration from the design and come up with your own personal creation.

YOU WILL NEED

Beads:
6 small gold or gold and enamel charms
6 x 8 mm-long green beads
6 x 2 mm pink seed beads
4 x 3 mm round silver beads

Findings:
kilt pin brooch finding with loops
5 lengths of fine chain varying
    from 2 to 3 inches (5–8 cm) long
8 x ¼ inch (6 mm) gold jump rings
3 x 1½ inch (4 cm) gold eye pins

Equipment:
round nose pliers
flat or bent nose pliers

Choose gold or silver
to match your
charm collection.

How to make a Magic Charm *Brooch*

Mix old charms and pendants with new findings and chain.

1 Open a jump ring with pliers and slip the last links of three lengths of chain onto the ring. Pass the ring through the first loop on the pin, add on a small charm, and fasten the jump ring as shown on page 28.

2 Fix the other two chains to a second jump ring, then attach the loose end of one of the first three chains through the ring. Add another small charm and secure the jump ring to the final loop on the pin.

*Choose eye pins a
similar color to
the pin and charms.*

③ Attach a small charm to the end of an eyepin (see page 31). Thread on a seed bead, a silver bead, a long green bead, another seed bead, a long bead, and a seed bead. Make a loop at the top of the pin, as on page 31, and attach the drop to the next loop on the pin with a jump ring.

④ Make another two long drops in the same way and fasten them to the pin with jump rings. Add a charm onto the jump ring of one of them. Finish off by fastening on the final charm.

TIP BOX

✳ If you cannot find a special finding with soldered loops like this, you can wire the charms onto an ordinary kilt pin or an extra large safety pin.

Beachcomber *Bracelet*

An antidote to the girlie projects in this book, this *surfer-style* bracelet is made from a leather cord and natural-look beads. Turn it into a vacation souvenir by adding a few SEASHELLS from your favorite beach to the tassels.

YOU WILL NEED

Beads:
2 x 10 mm-long cream cylindrical beads
35 x 6 mm-long cream cylindrical beads
12 mm-diameter pearl or bone button
8 x 8 mm flat cream beads
2 x 8 mm round brown beads
4 seashells with holes

Findings:
50 inches (130 cm) fine dark brown leather cord

Equipment:
scissors
(makes an 8-inch (20-cm) bracelet—alter the number of beads for a longer or shorter length)

These shells
were found on
a Fijian beach.

How to make a Beachcomber *Bracelet*

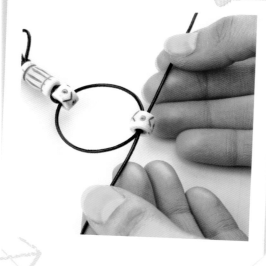

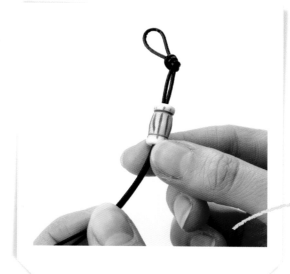

①   Fold the cord in half and tie an overhand knot ½ inch (13 mm) from the folded end to make the fastening loop. Pass both ends through one of the long, cylindrical beads.

②   Thread the end of the left-hand cord through the left side of a short cylindrical bead. Pass the right-hand cord through the right side of the hole. Pull up both ends tightly so that the bead sits just below the knot. Thread the remaining beads in the same way, keeping the loops taut and even, until the bracelet is the required length.

TIP BOX

If you fail to discover any shells with natural sea-worn holes when you are out beachcombing, you can buy them from specialty suppliers or bead stores.

(3) Thread the button onto one end of one cord, then make an overhand knot to keep it in place (see page 52). Pass both ends of the cord through the second long bead and make an overhand knot close to the bead.

(4) Knot one of the loose ends, approximately 2 inches (5 cm) from the button, and thread on a brown bead, four flat beads, and two shells. Tie a square knot to secure the shells and pass the cord back up through the beads. Trim the end. Finish the second cord to match.

See page 51 on how to tie a square knot.

Talisman *Choker*

Some beads are just so special that they need very little in the way of *extra adornment*. This choker is designed to showcase two ancient HAND-CARVED stone beads from Africa's Sahara Desert.

These beads were first worn many centuries ago.

YOU WILL NEED

Beads:
2 x special beads, one large and one small
4 x 1.5 mm-long cylindrical beads

Findings:
40 inches (1 m) fine cream leather cord
2 x leather crimp
1 x jump ring
1 x hook and eye clasp

Equipment:
scissors, bent or flat nose pliers

Leather cord
comes in lots
of other colors.

Use a larger
disc shaped bead
as the pendant.

How to make
a Talisman *Choker*

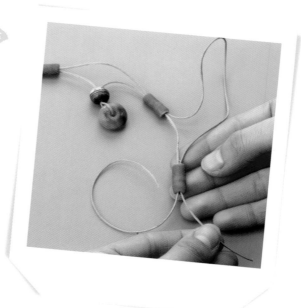

1 Cut the leather cord in half. Thread the large stone bead in the middle of one length, then pass both ends through the small bead.

2 Thread two cylindrical beads on either side of the center beads. Pass the second cord through all four cylindrical beads. Line up the ends of both cords.

TIP BOX

Look out for interesting clasps that reflect the individual character of the beads, rather than using an ordinary jump ring or lobster claw.

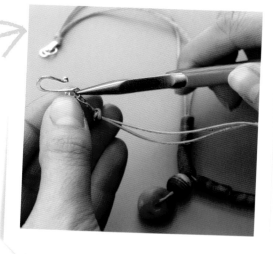

(3) Trim the cords so that the choker is the required length and knot them together at the ends. Attach a leather crimp to each pair of cords with pliers and trim the surplus cord.

(4) Attach a jump ring to one crimp and the necklace clasp to the other using the pliers (as shown on page 28).

Vintage *Earrings*

This is a chance to reuse those old broken NECKLACES from the bottom of your *jewelry box* and give them a new life.

Semiprecious beads are combined with shiny findings to give them a fresh new feel, while maintaining that vintage look.

YOU WILL NEED

Beads:
selection of old beads or broken necklaces and new beads to match. Allow 1 large crystal drop, and approximately 30 other small beads for each earring.

Findings:
2 silver bails or wire triangles
2 short silver eye pins
30 short silver head pins
pair of silver earring posts

Equipment:
wire cutters and round nose pliers

A cluster of beads
gives a modern look.

These faceted
drops will catch the
light beautifully.

How to make
Vintage *Earrings*

1   Carefully dismantle the jewelry, using
    wire cutters to remove any old wire.
Wash the beads in warm soapy water, rinse, and
place on some paper towels to dry.

2   Choose a long drop bead to form the
    lower part of the earring and fix a wire
triangule or bail through the hole. Attach the
loop of the eye pin through the bail.

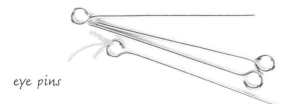

eye pins

4 Thread the droppers onto the eye pin, starting with the longest and positioning them carefully to form a cluster. Finish off with two small beads. Bend the end of the wire into a tight loop, and attach it to the earring fitting.

If you don't have old beads, use new.

3 Make fifteen droppers from a mixture of old and new beads, varying the length from ¼ to ½ inch (6–13 mm). For each one, thread two or more beads onto a head pin, trim the end to ¼ inch (6 mm), and bend the wire into a tight loop with the pliers.

Millefiori
Necklace

A new take on an old tradition, these contemporary versions of Venetian "THOUSAND FLOWER" beads are made from oven-hardening polymer clay, rather than *molten glass.*

Be warned—making these beads is a fascinating process —once you have started, you won't be able to stop!

YOU WILL NEED

Findings:
25-inch (66-cm) length of leather cord
2 x leather crimps
necklace clasp

Equipment:
1 packet each of polymer clay in
   coral, jade, and white
tile or plate for rolling the clay
craft knife
knitting needle

These chunky beads
would also look great
threaded on satin
cord or ribbon.

How to make a Millefiori *Necklace*

A cross section of the cane shows the floral pattern.

① Make eight 1½- x ⅛- inch (4 cm x 3 mm) rolls of clay, four white and four coral. Lay them out in a row and, alternating colors, gently press them together. Make a ¼-inch (6-mm) roll of jade clay and roll the striped piece around it.

② Make a ¹⁄₁₆ inch (1.5 mm) thick rectangle of jade clay, just large enough to cover the completed roll. Wrap it in place and roll out the cane with the tips of your fingers, until it is about ⅓ inch (8 mm) in diameter. Cut ¹⁄₁₆-inch (1.5-mm) slices from the cane with a craft knife.

3 Make a ball of coral clay about 1 inch (2.5 cm) in diameter for the foundation bead. Gently press the slices onto the surface of the ball, spacing them evenly. When it is covered, gently roll it between your palms until smooth.

TIP BOX

Polymer clay comes in a wide range of colors, but you can create your own shades by mixing two or more colors together. Knead the clay until it is soft before using.

4 Carefully push the knitting needle through the bead to make the hole, then pull it out. Bake the beads according to the manufacturer's instructions. When they are cool, thread them onto the cord. Attach leather crimps and a clasp to the two ends (see page 26).

Gemstone
Bobby Pins

It is said that every SEMIPRECIOUS STONE is endowed with *special powers*. Choose one (or more!) from the list below, wear your bobby pins every day, and enhance your well-being.

YOU WILL NEED

Beads:
9 x 2 mm seed beads
9 polished gemstone beads
    for each bobby pin

Findings:
60 inches (1.5 m) of 26-gauge wire
bobby pins

Equipment:
wire cutters, flat nose pliers
super glue

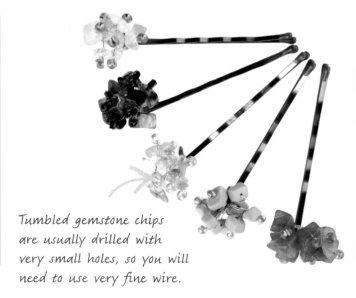

Tumbled gemstone chips are usually drilled with very small holes, so you will need to use very fine wire.

Choose seed beads that
complement the stones.

How to make a Gemstone *Bobby Pin*

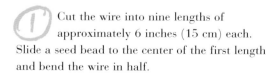

① Cut the wire into nine lengths of approximately 6 inches (15 cm) each. Slide a seed bead to the center of the first length and bend the wire in half.

② Pass both ends of the wire through a gemstone, then loop one strand back through the hole to keep it in place. Do the same with the remaining wires.

3 Group the wires together so that the gemstones form a "posy." Twist them together firmly to make a single strand.

THE MEANING OF GEMSTONES

amethyst—spirituality and contentment

green jade—physical and emotional peace

lapis lazuli—friendship and honesty

moonstone—emotional balance and intuition

quartz—healing and harmony

rose quartz—kindness and universal love

tigereye—self-discipline and patience

turquoise—peace of mind and loyalty

4 Loop the strand through the head of the bobby pin, leaving a ¼-inch (6 mm) stem between the pin and the posy. Twist the strands several times around the stem with the pliers, and trim. Glue the ends to stop them from unraveling.

Chain *Belt*

Make this ELEGANT, low-slung hipster belt

from the largest beads you can find, and

intersperse them with lengths of *antique-effect chain.*

Wear it informally with jeans or over a smart, loose dress.

YOU WILL NEED

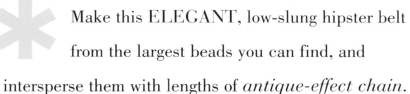

Beads:
5 x ½ inch (13 mm) flat glass, dark
    turquoise beads
7 x ½ inch (13 mm) flat glass, bronze beads
6 x 1 inch (2.5 cm) flat glass beads to match

Findings:
1 yard (1 m) of chain with ¼-inch (6-mm)
    wide links
lobster claw clasp with chain link
2 x ¼ inch (6 mm) jump rings
1 yard (1 m) of 22 gauge bronze craft wire

Equipment:
heavy-duty wire cutters.
bent or round nose pliers

This is a good project
to show off those larger,
more expensive beads.

How to make a Chain *Belt*

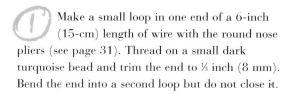

① Make a small loop in one end of a 6-inch (15-cm) length of wire with the round nose pliers (see page 31). Thread on a small dark turquoise bead and trim the end to ⅓ inch (8 mm). Bend the end into a second loop but do not close it.

② Cut fourteen 1¼ inch (3 cm) lengths of chain. Slip the end of one piece onto the open loop and close it with the pliers. Wire up a small bronze bead and attach one loop to the end of the chain. Continue adding lengths of chain and alternate large flat glass and small bronze beads until the belt is complete, ending with a second dark turquoise bead.

3   Use the pliers to attach the lobster claw clasp and a jump ring to the remaining loop on the final bead.

TIP BOX

The instructions are for a belt approximately 30 inches (80 cm) long. Add more chain and beads to make a longer version.

4   Cut three lengths of chain, 4 inches (10 cm), 3½ inches (9 cm), and 3 inches (8 cm) long. Wire the remaining three beads and fix one to the end of each chain. Join the other ends together with a jump ring and slip on the fastening chain. Attach the ring to the loop on the first bead.

Flower
Power

Flower
Hair *Comb*

This floral corsage for your hair is a great way to transform your old TREASURES: It is created from a mixture of new *glass beads* and the remains of a broken necklace, all in toning shades of blue.

Bell caps are usually used to embellish large beads.

YOU WILL NEED

Beads:
10 x 2.5 cm-long dark blue beads
25 x 3 mm clear blue seed beads
3 x 6 mm clear faceted beads
6 x 2.5 cm long light blue beads

Findings:
2 yards (2 m) of 24 gauge dark blue craft wire
3 x filigree metal bead cups

Equipment:
wire cutters
4-inch (10-mm) wide black hair comb
8-inch (20-cm) strip of double-sided adhesive tape
39 inches (1 m) of 3/16-inch (4-mm) wide black velvet ribbon
clear glue

Attach the same
flowers to a barrette
for a change.

How to make a Flower *Hair Comb*

1 Cut a 20-inch (50-cm) length of wire. Thread a seed bead onto the center, then pass both ends through a large blue bead. Thread a second bead and a seed bead onto one end. Pass the wire down through the bead. Repeat once more, then twice on the other end.

2 Twist the wire together and wrap both ends several times over and under the base of the beads. Pass one end up through the center. Thread on a filigree cup and a faceted bead. Take the wire back down and twist the ends together twice. Make another similar flower and a six-petaled light blue flower.

TIP BOX

✳ This comb uses recycled vintage beads from old jewelry, so any interpretation of the steps will be completely individual. It is designed to inspire you to create your own version using your own selection of larger glass beads.

③ Make four small flowers in the same way, each made up of three beads from the old necklace, three seed beads, and a 6-inch (16-cm) length of wire. These will go at the edges of the comb and between the large flowers.

④ Stick double-sided tape along the front and back of the comb top. Fix the flowers in place by wrapping each end of the wire twice around the top and twisting the ends together. Trim the ends and press them along the top of the comb. Wrap the ribbon around the top to conceal the wire, passing it between the teeth of the comb. Glue down the ends at the back.

Beaded
Barrettte

There is so much more you can do with beads than simple threading! Here they have been WIRED INTO FLOWERS and wrapped around a simple barrette to make a *dazzling* hair accessory—make more than one for a display.

Rose montees are rhinestones with metal backing.

YOU WILL NEED

Beads:
around 50 x 7 mm silver bugle beads
five 2-cm long, clear oval glass beads
2 x 8 mm sew-on rose montees

Findings:
³/₈-inch (1-cm) wide barrette finding
36 inches (94 cm) of 26-gauge silver wire

Equipment:
wire cutters
bent nose or flat nose pliers
clear adhesive or nail polish
4 inches (10 cm) ³/₈-inch (1-cm) wide ribbon

Wear flowers in
your hair whatever
the weather.

How to make a Beaded *Barrette*

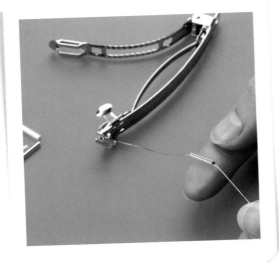

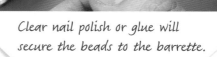

Clear nail polish or glue will secure the beads to the barrette.

1 Cut a 20-inch (50-cm) length of wire. Open the barrette and fasten one end of the wire securely to the bottom left corner of the top part. Thread on a bugle bead and push it down to the end of the wire.

2 Wind the wire over the barrette so that the bead sits on the top, at right angles, then bring it out again at the bottom edge. Thread on another bead, then continue wrapping beads to the end. Attach the final bead to the barrette and then adhere with clear glue or nail polish.

This smaller barrette uses different colors and a button.

③ Thread a clear bead onto the center of the remaining wire. Twist the ends together with pliers, then thread on two more beads on each side, twisting the wire at the base of each. Twist the loose ends together to make a flower.

TIP BOX

For a really dazzling look for that one-of-a-kind social event, you could make two more bead flowers and attach them to large clip-on earring backings or bobby pins.

④ Take one end of the wire to the front and thread on a rose montee. Push the wire to the back, then do the same with the other end. Twist the loose ends together, then wrap them around the center top of the barrette. Tuck under the sharp ends, then glue a length of ribbon along the underside to hide any sharp ends of wire.

Spring Flower
Necklace

This delicate, FLOWERY NECKLACE will set off your prettiest summer dress to perfection. It is made from three strands of frosted glass beads and cute *daisy-shaped sequins*, interspersed with lengths of springy French wire all on nylon-coated wire.

YOU WILL NEED

Beads:
30 x 8 mm green matte glass beads
30 x 6 mm turquoise matte glass beads
120 x flower-shaped sequins in matching colors
2 x clamshell crimps

Findings:
3 x 10-inch lengths of French wire in matt white, purple, and metallic purple

90-inch length x 0.15 tigertail wire
2 x jump rings
1 x lobster claw fastener

Equipment:
wire cutters
adhesive tape
bent or flat nose pliers

French wire is hollow, so
when cut into lengths you
can use them like beads.

How to make
a Spring Flower *Necklace*

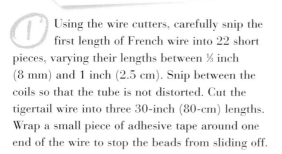

You should be able to thread tigertail without using a needle.

1) Using the wire cutters, carefully snip the first length of French wire into 22 short pieces, varying their lengths between ⅓ inch (8 mm) and 1 inch (2.5 cm). Snip between the coils so that the tube is not distorted. Cut the tigertail wire into three 30-inch (80-cm) lengths. Wrap a small piece of adhesive tape around one end of the wire to stop the beads from sliding off.

2) Thread a piece of French wire, a sequin, a green bead, and another matching sequin onto the first length of tigertail. Continue threading, repeating this pattern until there is just 2 inches (5 cm) of wire left. Finish off with a piece of French wire and another piece of tape to secure the beads.

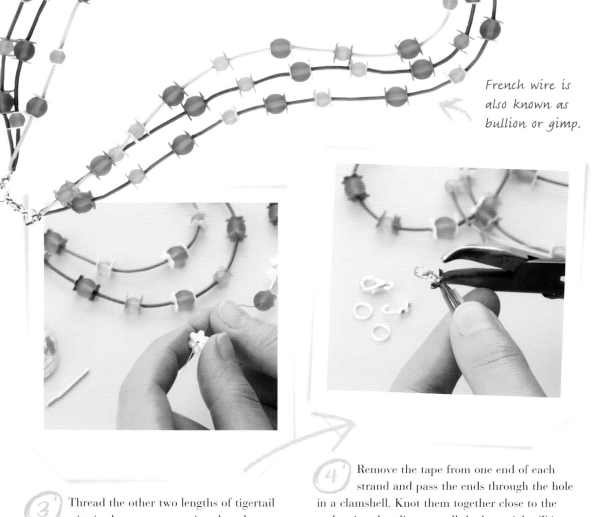

French wire is also known as bullion or gimp.

3 Thread the other two lengths of tigertail wire in the same way, using the other two pieces of French wire to space the beads. Thread one until there are 2¾ inches (7 cm) at the end and the other until there is 3½ inches (9 cm) left, so the three strands will be different lengths.

4 Remove the tape from one end of each strand and pass the ends through the hole in a clamshell. Knot them together close to the end, using the pliers to pull the knot tight. Trim, then slide up the clamshell, squeezing it shut with pliers. Do the same with the other ends, then attach a jump ring to each clamshell and a lobster claw clasp to one ring, as shown on page 28.

Vintage Rose *Corsage*

Add a touch of SHABBY CHIC to your wardrobe with this gorgeous rose corsage. Its tweed and velvet petals are embellished with rounds of seed beads and a *sprinkling* of colored rose montees.

YOU WILL NEED

Beads:
½ ounce of 3 mm silver-lined pale gold seed beads
10 x 6 mm sew-on rose montees in coordinating colors
5-inch (12.5-cm) square of fine tweed fabric to match

Findings:
24-inch length (61-cm) of 24 gauge bronze craft wire

1 x 1¼-inch (6 cm) diameter pierced brooch backing

Equipment:
wire cutters
needle nose pliers
pinking shears
size 10 sewing needle
matching sewing thread
a velvet or silk rose
2 x sprays of fabric rose leaves

Rose montees on
the leaves look
like drops of dew.

How to make
a Vintage Rose *Corsage*

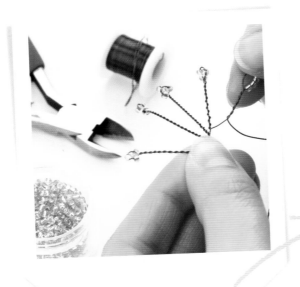

1 Thread three seed beads onto the wire, 2 inches (5 cm) from the end. Bend the ends down and twist them together by hand for 1 inch (2.5 cm) to make the first stamen. Repeat eleven more times, then twist the two loose ends together. Trim, and turn under the sharp ends with pliers.

2 Dismantle the rose and snip the petals apart. Pick out three small petals and eight large ones. Using a large petal as a guide, cut out five tweed petal shapes with pinking shears. Sew a line of beads around each one about ¼ inch (6 mm) from the edge.

TIP BOX

If you cannot find a suitable fabric flower, cut out large and small petals from a fragment of old velvet or brocade.

4 Sew the two leaf sprays to the back of the rose. Stitch the finished piece onto the front part of the brooch backing. passing the needle backward and forward through the holes so that it is secure. Fit the backing in place, and secure the clips with pliers.

3 Stitch a sprinkling of rose montees onto a few of the petals and the leaves. Wrap the base of a small petal around the bottom of the stamens, and stitch it securely in place. Add the next two small petals, overlapping them so that they surround the stamens. Sew on the five tweed petals, then the large fabric petals, stitching through the base of all the petals to form the rose.

Guardian *Angel*

This *ethereal* angel is bound to bring good fortune to everyone she meets: Make one for yourself and another for your BEST FRIEND, cross your fingers, close your eyes, and make a wish!

Make a whole host of angels.

YOU WILL NEED

Beads:
½ ounce (15 g) 3 mm silver-lined seed beads

Equipment:
15 inches (40 cm) of 20 gauge craft wire
30 inches (80 cm) of 24 gauge silver craft wire
scissors

hot-glue gun
wire cutters
round nose pliers
wooden clothespin
red and black ballpoint pens
white silk flower
6 x white feathers
1 x ½ inch- (1.5 cm-) diameter velvet flower

Angels will make
stylish Christmas
tree decorations

How to make a Guardian *Angel*

Draw a serene face for your angel.

1 Cut eight ¼-inch (6 mm) lengths from the feather tips and glue around the head, with the velvet flower in the center. For the tiara, thread a seed bead 1 inch (2.5 cm) from the end of a 6-inch (15-cm) length of fine wire. Twist the wire for ⅓ inch (8 mm). Thread another bead ⅔ inch (1.5 cm) further along and twist to make the second point, leaving ¼ inch (6 mm) untwisted.

2 Repeat this twisting five more times, then twist the wire to fit. To make the skirt, dismantle the silk flower and choose two rounds of petals. Enlarge the center holes to ⅓ inch (8 mm) and glue them in place. Glue the feathers under the petals, positioning them so that they all turn outward.

③ For the bodice, thread approximately 8 inches (20 cm) of beads onto the remaining fine wire, bending back the ends so they do not slip off. Apply a thin layer of glue to the top of the clothespin. Wrap the beads around the waist and over the glue. Trim and neaten the ends.

*Someone
to watch
over you.*

④ Twist one end of the thicker wire into a small loop with round nose pliers. Thread seed beads along the wire to within ½ inch (2.5 cm) of the end. Slip the loose end through the loop and secure with the pliers. Twist the wire into a wing shape and glue to the angel's back.

Rosette

You can create this *delicate*, lacy motif from colored tigertail and softly gleaming crystal beads in just a few minutes. Stitch it onto a floaty scarf, tie it around your neck, and WEAR IT with panache.

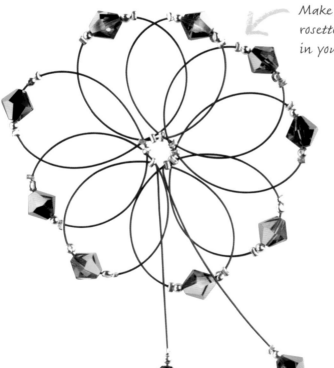

Make another rosette to wear in your hair.

YOU WILL NEED

Beads:
11 x 8 mm bicone crystal beads
22 x 2 mm silver round beads
22 silver crimp beads

Equipment:
40 inches (1 m) of tigertail
    or nylon-coated wire
bent nose or crimping pliers

Black crystals are
both sophisticated
and glamorous.

How to make a *Rosette*

② Squeeze the crimp with the pliers. Hold the loop upside down so that the beads fall to the bottom and close the other two crimps to hold them in this central position.

① Thread two crimps, a silver bead, a bicone crystal, a silver bead, and another crimp onto the tigertail, approximately 4 inches (10.5 cm) from the right end. Pass the left end back through the first crimp and draw it up to form a loop of about 3 inches (8 cm).

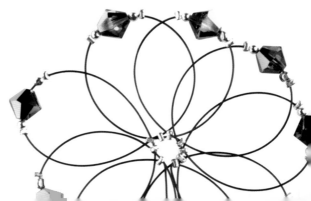

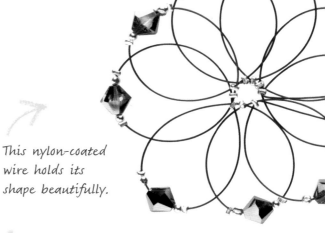

This nylon-coated wire holds its shape beautifully.

(3) Repeat these two steps eight more times to make a series of overlapping loops, like the petals of a flower.

TIP BOX

This is a pretty and versatile project: You could glue the finished rosette onto a stickpin finding and wear it on your lapel or sew it onto a pale evening bag.

(4) Finish off by attaching a crimp, a silver bead, a bicone, another silver bead, and a second crimp to each loose end. Secure the crimps.

Putting

on

the Glitz

Rhinestone
Jacket

Enhance the *classic* lines of a denim jacket with simple beading—rows of dazzling ROSE MONTEE crystals and a scattering of Indian silver sequins. Why not use up any leftover beads by trimming your jeans to match?

Paillettes are sequins with more holes.

YOU WILL NEED

Beads:
22 x 7 mm sew-on rhinestones
    or rose montees
70 x 5 mm sew-on rose montees
¼ ounce (10 g) 2 mm mixed metallic
    blue seed beads
70 x light blue cup sequins
50 x paillettes in assorted shapes
70 x silver cup sequins

Materials:
denim jacket
matching sewing thread

Equipment:
thimble
size 8 sewing needle

Dress up your
casual denim
with sequins.

How to make a Rhinestone *Jacket*

rose montees

1 Sew seven large rose montees around the edge of each pocket flap between the lines of stitching. To space them evenly, sew one at the point, one at each corner, and one at each top edge, then add three more at regular intervals in both remaining spaces.

2 Decorate the two vertical front seams with rows of alternate small diamantes and blue cup sequins held in place with a seed bead. You will need to use a thimble to push the needle through all the layers of fabric.

3 Block in the area between the two beaded seams with the shaped sequins and paillettes. Sew them on with a small stitch through each hole at the edge or with a seed bead if there is a central hole.

4 Add a few silver cup sequins, each one secured with a seed bead to fill in the spaces left between the larger sequins.

Stitch twice through each hole for strength.

Remember that the finished jacket can be dry-cleaned only.

Pinup Print
T-shirt

bugles

Turn a plain T-shirt into a FUNKY GARMENT by adding a trio of 1920s bathing beauties. The image, which comes from a vintage postcard discovered in a French *flea market,* is embellished with starbursts of sequins, beads, and rose montees.

YOU WILL NEED

Beads:
5 x 8 mm green rose montees
30 x pink cup sequins
90 x 3 mm silver-lined pink seed beads
30 x 12 mm green bugles
60 x 3 mm silver-lined green seed beads

Materials:
3 photos or old postcards
iron-on photo transfer paper
white T-shirt
white sewing cotton

Equipment:
scissors, iron
fine sewing needle

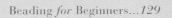

Use photographs of friends for a personal present.

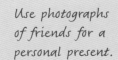

How to make a Pinup Print *T-Shirt*

1 Wash and press the T-shirt. Photocopy or scan the three images onto transfer paper and cut each one out close to the edge. Iron them onto the front of the shirt, following the manufacturer's instructions carefully.

2 To make the first star, sew a green rose montee at the bottom right-hand corner of the lowest image. Add a circle of six pink sequins around the rose montee, each anchored by a pink seed bead.

3 Bring up the needle in between two of the sequins. Thread on a bugle, a pink seed bead, and a green seed bead, then take the needle back down so that they lie in a straight line. Come back up at the edge of the sequin to the left and sew on a pink and a green seed bead. Continue in this way around the star.

4 Sew four more stars along the center front of the T-shirt, positioning them at the corners of the other images. Hand wash the shirt when necessary in cool, soapy water and dry flat.

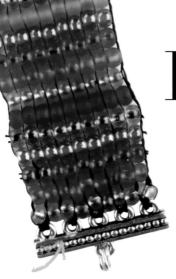

Loom-woven *Bracelet*

Weaving on a loom does not have to be tricky: This bracelet is made from extra-large SEED BEADS so it is a good project to try if you are new to the *technique*.

Choose pretty findings to match your color scheme.

YOU WILL NEED

Beads:
54 x 4 mm seedbeads in six colors: silver-lined gold, iridescent orange, pink-lined clear, matte orange, matte red, matte gold

Findings:
bracelet clasp with five loops
2 x ⅛ inch (4 mm) jump rings
bolt ring clasp

Equipment:
beading loom
scissors
measuring tape or ruler
reel of black Nymo thread
long beading needle and sewing needle

Most women have a wrist size of around 7 inches (18 cm). Check your measurement and take away ½ inch (13 mm) for the width of the clasp

Larger beads mean
that the bracelet
will grow quickly.

How to make a Loom-Woven *Bracelet*

The warp stays along the length, and the weft travels across.

① Cut ten 20-inch (52 cm) lengths of Nymo for the warp. Knot them together in a bunch at each end, then divide into two groups of five. Slip the knots over the pins at each end of the loom, then turn the rollers so the threads wind around them and become taut. Tighten the screws and slot the threads between the coils of wire to space them evenly.

② Tie a 30-inch (80 cm) length of thread to the first thread on the left, leaving a 2-inch tail. Thread a beading needle onto the other end and picking up nine beads in the first color, take them from left to right under the warp. Push the beads up with your index finger so one sits in each of the spaces between the warp. Pass the needle back through the beads and over the warp threads.

Looped clasps and spacers come in many finishes.

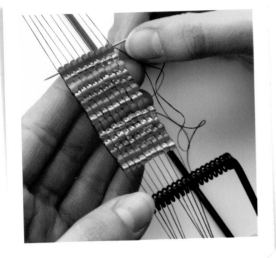

③ Continue adding more rows of beads in this way, catching the tail of the weft under the thread as you pass it from left to right. Repeat the same sequence of beads until the bracelet is the required length. If you come to the end of the weft, weave the end back several times through the beads and tie on a new one as before. Wind the rollers around if you run out of space.

④ Remove the finished piece from the loom and untie the warp. Tie the thread together in pairs so the beads stay in place. Sew each pair of threads onto a loop of the fastening with a sewing needle, passing them back into the bracelet to make the join strong. Attach a jump ring and half of the clasp to each end of the fastening.

Ice Queen
Tiara

This SHIMMERING TIARA is great fun to make and glamorous to wear. Create different *icicle-like spines* using your own selection of beads and crystals and following the ideas here.

Choose your own color scheme to match your outfit.

YOU WILL NEED

Beads:
selection of clear, iridescent, and silver beads in various sizes, including seed beads, bugles, faceted beads, and crystals

Findings:
6 yards (5.5 m) of 26-gauge silver wire
silver head pins
narrow metal headband
silver crimps

Equipment:
15 inches (40 cm) of ribbon, the same width as headband
wire cutters,
flat nose pliers and round nose pliers

Great for a prom
queen, or to hold on
your wedding veil.

How to make an Ice Queen *Tiara*

1   To make a branched spine, thread a seed bead to the center of a 6-inch (16 cm) length of wire, then pass both ends through two bugle beads. Thread another bugle and a seed bead onto one end, then pass the wire back through the bugle. Thread both ends through three more bugles and a crimp. Squeeze the crimp firmly with pliers.

2   For a hanging drop spine, bend a 6-inch (16 cm) length of wire in half and use round nose pliers to make a loop at the fold. Thread a short row of beads onto both ends and secure with a crimp. Attach a large and a small crystal to a head pin to make a hanging drop and bend the end with round nose pliers. Slip the wire over the loop and close it with flat nose pliers.

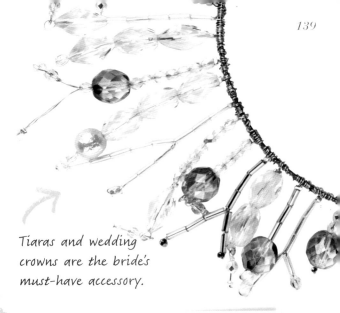

Tiaras and wedding crowns are the bride's must-have accessory.

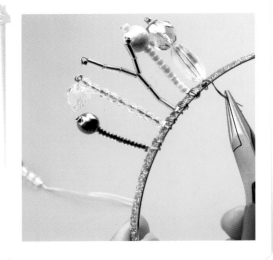

3 The straight spines are made by threading a seed bead to the center of a 6-inch (16 cm) piece of wire, then passing both ends through large, medium, or small beads. Attach them with a crimp, as in step one.

4 Fix the spines in place by binding both ends of the wire around the hairband, using pliers to pull them tightly. Trim the loose ends and push them back into the coiled wire. Glue a narrow strip of ribbon to the underside of the band to conceal them completely.

Bag *Charm*

Far more than just a simple key ring—this PINK CONFECTION doubles up as a *zipper pull* on your favorite bag or you could fix it onto a brooch backing or even a hair scrunchie.

The beads are linked with wire hoops.

YOU WILL NEED

Beads:
10 x 7 mm pink glass beads
7 x 7 mm turquoise glass beads
6 x large beads to match, each
        12 mm or longer

Findings:
24 inches (61 cm) of 20 gauge
        silver-plated wire
3 x ⅓ inch (8 mm) silver jump rings
1 x ½ inch (12 mm) silver jump ring
1 x 1 inch (25 mm) silver split ring

Equipment:
wire cutters
round nose pliers and flat nose pliers

Large split rings are
used for key rings.

How to make a Bag *Charm*

1 Cut a length of wire approximately 3 inches (8 cm) long and, using the round nose pliers, make a small loop at one end (see page 31). Thread on four or five beads, then trim the end of the wire to ⅓ inch (8 mm). Bend it back in a loop with the pliers.

2 Make a loop at the end of a 1-inch (2.5-cm) length of wire and thread on a round bead. Bend the other end around, and just before closing, slip it through the loop at the top of the long drop. Add on two to four more beads to form a chain.

TIP BOX

✳ The basic wiring technique used to join the single beads into a chain is a good way to show off a few pretty beads, and it can easily be used to make a bracelet or necklace.

3 Make another two drops, varying the length from around 3 to 4 inches (8–10.5 cm), then attach a small jump ring to the top of each one using flat nose pliers.

4 Join all three drops together with the large jump ring, then attach this to the split ring.

Heart & Star *Rings*

These sweet rings are SURPRISINGLY straightforward and make a great introduction to needle weaving. You can quickly create a *whole handful*, each in a different color scheme.

The rings are made using a simple threading technique.

YOU WILL NEED

Findings:
24 inches (60 cm) fine nylon
 beading thread

Beads:
2 x 4 mm fire-polished faceted oval beads
29 x 2 mm pink seed beads
1 x 8 mm pink star-shaped bead
4 x 4 mm pink round beads
1 x 4 mm clear round bead

Equipment:
super glue, scissors

The shanks on the underside use a double strand of seed beads.

How to make
Heart & Star
Rings

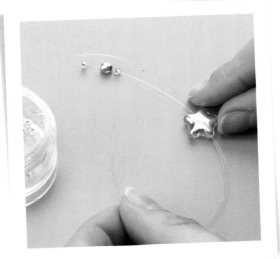

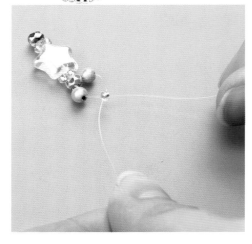

1. Thread a fire-polished bead along to the center of the thread and add a pink seed bead on either side. Pass both ends through the star-shaped bead.

2. Thread another seed bead onto each end and pass both ends through another fire-polished bead. Thread a round pink bead on each end and pass both ends through a seed bead. Pull up both ends tightly.

Our rings are in pastel shades, but you can use any range of colors.

3 To make the shank (the part that goes around the back of your finger) put six seed beads onto each end and pass them both through the clear round bead.

TIP BOX

If you need to make the ring larger, you can add more seed beads to the shank in steps 3 and 4. If the ring needs to be smaller, add fewer beads.

4 Add another six seed beads and a round pink bead to each end. To complete the ring, thread one end through the first fire-polished bead and tie a tight knot. Put a dab of glue over the knot. Pass the nylon back through all of the beads before trimming the ends.

Crystal
Snowflake

Increase the *sophistication* of your seasonal decorations with a crystal snowflake. The ready-made wire forms are available in several sizes, so you could go on to make a whole flurry to hang from your CHRISTMAS TREE branches.

YOU WILL NEED

Beads:
6 x 3 mm clear seed beads
12 x 4 mm turquoise oval faceted beads
6 x 8 mm lilac oval faceted beads
6 x 8 mm iridescent oval crystal beads
12 x 8 mm turquoise and lilac round glass beads
6 x 8 mm-diameter clear faceted rondelles
6 x 12 mm iridescent oval crystal beads

Findings:
1 x 6-inch 6-point wire form

Equipment:
round nose pliers
10-inch (25-cm) length of clear thread

Crystals will catch
the winter light at
your window.

How to make
a Crystal *Snowflake*

1. Thread a seed bead, a turquoise oval bead, and a lilac oval bead onto the first wire arm. Add on a small iridescent crystal, a round turquoise and lilac bead, a rondelle, a large crystal, a second round turquoise and lilac bead, and a second turquoise oval bead.

2. Using the tip of the pliers, bend the remaining wire gently backward at an angle. Move the wire further down the jaws of the pliers and squeeze them together to close the loop.

TIP BOX

As a variation, you could mix round and teardrop pearls with the crystal beads or add rhinestone rondelles between the beads.

3 Do the same with the remaining five arms of the snowflake, keeping the sequence of beads the same on each one so that it will be symmetrical.

4 To make a hanging loop, pass one end of the clear thread through one of the wire loops and tie the two ends together securely with an overhand knot.

Turquoise Jewel
Bracelet

This SUMPTUOUS bracelet is woven using an easy-to-learn technique that simply means that beads are threaded onto *two strands* of thread, rather than the usual one.

YOU WILL NEED

Beads:
72 x 3 mm dark turquoise bugle beads
8 x 4 mm clear bicone crystals
38 x 2 mm turquoise seed bead beads
2 x 4 mm faceted clear oval beads
8 x 4 mm blue bicone crystals
2 x 4 mm faceted white oval beads
8 x 4 mm iridescent clear seed bead beads
2 x 8 mm turquoise oval beads
8 x 4 mm dark turquoise round beads
2 x 8 mm ridged metallic turquoise bead

1 x 2 cm large oval turquoise glass bead
1 x 8 mm turquoise oval drop bead

Findings:
50 inches (1.3 m) of fine nylon beading thread
2 x small clamshells
spring ring and extender chain clasp

Equipment:
adhesive tape
needle nose pliers

Choose interestingly shaped beads
in a similarly close tonal range
when making your own version.

How to make a Turquoise Jewel *Bracelet*

1 Fold the thread in half and wrap a short length of adhesive tape over the top end, making a 1 ½ inch (4 cm) loop. Thread six bugles and a bicone crystal onto each end. Thread a turquoise seed bead onto one end, then pass the other end through it as well. Thread another bicone crystal onto each end.

2 Add two turquoise seed beads to each end, then pass both ends through a clear oval bead. Put two seed beads and a blue bicone on each end and thread them both through a white seed bead. Thread another bicone and two seed beads on each end and pass both through an oval white faceted bead. Put two turquoise seed beads and an iridescent bead on each end, pass both ends through a turquoise seed bead, and thread an iridescent bead and two bugles on each end. Pass them both through an oval turquoise bead.

3   Thread two bugles and a round metallic turquoise bead on each end, pass both ends through a turquoise seed bead, and add another dark turquoise round bead and two bugles to each end. Thread both ends through a ridged turquoise bead and add two more bugles. Pass both ends through the large center bead and thread two bugles onto each one.

With an extender chain, the bracelet should fit any size.

4   Work the second half of the bracelet in the same way, reversing the order of the weave so that it forms a mirror image. Pass the two ends through a crimp. Knot and glue the threads as shown on page 28, then remove the tape from the loop and do the same at the other end. Fix the drop bead to the end of the chain, then use pliers to fasten the chain to one crimp and the jump ring to the other.

Pearls and *Crystals*

The stylish pairing of pearls and sparkling CRYSTALS gives this matching bracelet and earrings set a classic elegance. The beads were salvaged from *vintage finds*, so search for your own unique treasure.

YOU WILL NEED

FOR THE BRACELET

Beads:
A selection of pearl and crystal beads:
allow 2 or 3 beads for each pin

Findings:
1 x 1-inch (2.5-cm) long silver head pin and
    small silver jump ring for each pin
chain bracelet

Equipment:
round nose pliers and flat nose pliers

FOR THE EARRINGS

Beads:
2 small beads, 4 medium crystals,
    and 2 large crystals

Findings:
2 x long silver head pins
pair of ball and post earring findings

Freshwater pearls have a
roughness that contrasts
with the sharper crystals.

How to make Pearls and *Crystals*

To make each drop, thread two or three beads onto a head pin leaving at least ¼ inch (7 mm) at the end. Bend the top of the wire into a loop with the round nose pliers, as shown on page 31.

Open up a jump ring (see page 28). Slip the head pin loop onto the ring, then fasten the jump ring onto the second link of the chain with flat, or bent nose, pliers.

Use the beads you have left to make matching drops.

③ Continue fixing the drops onto every other link until the bracelet is complete. Alternate the colors and shapes of each charm as you go so that it looks varied and interesting.

TIP BOX

To calculate how many jump rings and head pins you will need, count the number of links in the bracelet and divide by two.

④ Thread one large crystal, two medium crystals, and then a small crystal onto a long head pin. Bend the top of the wire into a loop. Open out the bottom loop of the finding and slip the earring in place. Use the pliers to close the loop once again.

Index

By browsing the internet you can discover an enormous range of stores across the world, who will deliver every imaginable bead to your doorstep. Here are just a few of the best and the most unusual websites:

www.affordablebeading.com;
www.allseedbeads.com;
www.beadbazaar.co.nz;
www.bead-world.com;
www.brightlingsbeads.com ;
www.brucefrankbeads.com;
www.ebeadshop.com ; www.honey-beads.com; www.indiabead.com;
www.jewelrysupply.com; www.london-beadco.co.uk; www.matoska.com;
www.shipwreck.com; www.thebead-site.com; www.venetianbeadshop.com;
www.2bead.com; www.africantrade-beads.com; www.beadykate.com.